On a blue planet lived a little prince and a beautiful rose. The rose was the prince's only friend and he loved her very much.

But the rose was too proud and temperamental and the little prince began to find her tiresome.

One day, the little prince was so annoyed with the rose that he left his planet, hoping to find some new friends elsewhere.

Hoping to find news friends, the little prince went to another planet. There he met an arrogant and overbearing King, who was sitting on a great throne.

The King appointed the little prince Minister of Justice. He ordered his new Minister to sentence a rat to death.

Unwilling to give the poor rat the death penalty, the little prince left and continued on his journey to find new friends.

The little prince arrived at a second planet where he met a very vain person.

The vain person insisted that the little prince clap his hands to applaud and admire him.

The little prince was asked to do this over and over again. In the end, he couldn't stand it any longer so he left for another planet.

The little prince reached a third planet. There he met a person who spent all his time eating and drinking.

The little prince asked the man, "Why do you eat and drink so much?" The man answered, "Because it helps me forget my sadness."

"You eat and drink so much just to forget your sadness? That's nonsense!" said the little prince, and he felt very disappointed and left again.

The little prince landed on a fourth planet where he met a businessman who only cared about money.

The little prince asked, "How much money would you need to be satisfied?" The businessman replied greedily, "Enough to own all of the stars in the sky!"

The little prince didn't want to have anything to do with this greedy businessman, so he set off for the next planet.

Soon the little prince arrived at a fifth planet. The planet was so tiny that it was only big enough for a lamp and the person who looked after it.

The person's job was to light the lamp at night and put it out in the morning. The job kept him very busy. The little prince thought he might be a good friend.

However, the planet was too small to fit another person. Reluctantly, the little prince waved goodbye to the man.

The little prince landed on a sixth planet. A geographer, who lived there, encouraged the little prince to go and try his luck on Earth.

The Little Prince set off to visit Earth. It looked like a blue diamond and he hoped he could find some new friends there.

Finally the little prince arrived on Earth. Unlike all the other planets he had visited, there were lots of people on it and everyone was different.

The little prince was very disappointed to discover that, even amongst so many people, he couldn't find any good friends.

Having travelled so far, the little prince began to miss his own planet and his friend, the rose. So he left Earth and headed back to his own planet.

The little prince returned to his own planet where he finally realised that the beautiful rose was truly his best friend. He lived happily with his friend ever after.